Experiments
with
SOUND

Isabel Thomas

heinemann
raintree

To contact Capstone Global Library, please call
800-747-4992, or visit our web site www.capstonepub.com

Edited by Clare Lewis and Amanda Robbins
Designed by Steve Mead
Picture research by Eric Gohl
Production by Victoria Fitzgerald
Originated by Capstone Global Library Ltd
Printed and bound by CTPS in China

19 18 17 16 15 14
10 9 8 7 6 5 4 3 2 1

Library of Congress Cataloging-in-Publication Data
Thomas, Isabel, 1979- author.
  Experiments with sound / Isabel Thomas.
     pages cm.—(Read and experiment)
  Summary: "Explore the world of sound with engaging text,
real life examples and fun step-by-step experiments. This
book brings the science of sound to life, explaining the con-
cepts then getting kids to be hands-on scientists!"—Provided
by the publisher.
  Includes bibliographical references and index.
  ISBN 978-1-4109-6836-4 (hb)—ISBN 978-1-4109-7900-1 (pb)—
ISBN 978-1-4109-6841-8 (ebook) 1. Sound—Experiments—Juvenile literature. 2. Sound—Juvenile literature. I. Title.

  QC225.5.T53 2015
  534.078—dc23   2014016071

This book has been officially leveled by using the F&P Text
Level Gradient™ Leveling System.

Acknowledgments

We would like to thank the following for permission to
reproduce photographs: NASA: 16; Newscom: Minden
Pictures/Pete Oxford, 15, Reuters/Stringer, 18; Shutterstock:
Andrey_Popov, 10, Bryan Brazil, 22 (right), Monkey Business
Images, 11 (bottom)

All other photographs were created at Capstone Studio by
Karon Dubke.

We would like to thank Patrick O'Mahony for his invaluable
help in the preparation of this book.

Every effort has been made to contact copyright holders
of material reproduced in this book. Any omissions will
be rectified in subsequent printings if notice is given to
the publisher.

Safety instructions for adult helper
The experiments in this book should be planned and carried out with adult supervision. Certain steps should
only be carried out by an adult – these are indicated in the text. Always follow the instructions carefully, and
be extra careful when using scissors (pg. 12) and glass bottles (pg. 24). Never poke fingers or any other object
into your ears. Never make loud noises near your ears. The publisher and author disclaim, to the maximum
extent possible, all liability for any accidents, injuries or losses that may occur as a result of the information or
instructions in this book.

Contents

Some words are shown in bold, **like this**. You can find out what they mean by looking in the glossary.

Why Experiment?

Why is space silent? How can blue whales hear each other hundreds of miles apart? Why do some animals have enormous ears? You can answer all these questions by investigating sound.

Scientists ask questions like these. They find the answers with the help of **experiments**.

Get your ears, eyes, and hands ready! You'll need to **observe** your experiments carefully and record what you hear, see, or feel.

An experiment is a test that has been carefully planned to help answer a question.

The experiments in this book will help you to understand what sound is and how it behaves. You'll learn how to work like a scientist, and have lots of fun along the way!

IS IT A FAIR TEST?

Most experiments involve changing something to see what happens. Make sure you only change one thing, or **variable**, at a time. Then you will know that it was the variable you changed that made the difference. This is called a fair test.

WARNING! Ask an adult to help you plan and carry out each experiment. Follow the instructions carefully. Look out for this sign.

ADULT HELP

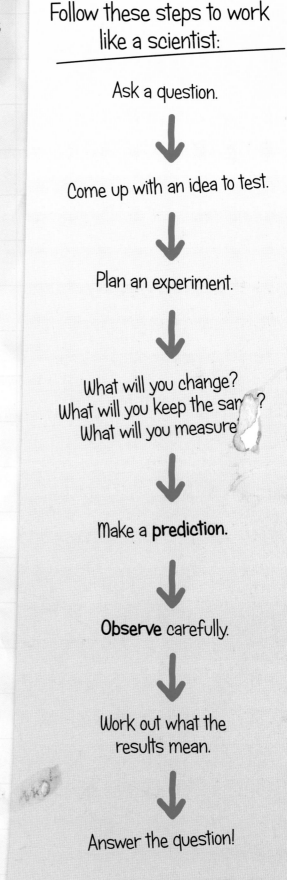

Follow these steps to work like a scientist:

Ask a question.

↓

Come up with an idea to test.

↓

Plan an experiment.

↓

What will you change? What will you keep the same? What will you measure?

↓

Make a **prediction**.

↓

Observe carefully.

↓

Work out what the results mean.

↓

Answer the question!

What Is Sound?

Sounds are made when something **vibrates** (moves back and forth). The vibrations are passed through the air as **sound waves**. When the vibrations reach our ears, we hear them as sounds.

Turn on a radio and hold a balloon near the speaker, without touching it. Can you feel vibrations?

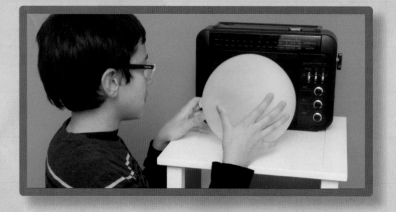

The speaker vibrates backwards and forwards. As it moves, it pushes the air around it. This air is squished out of the way, and pushes the air next to it. The vibrations are passed on from one part of the air to the next. When they reach the balloon, they make the balloon and the air inside vibrate, too.

Sound waves move through the air a bit like pressure from your hands moves through a slinky. Stretch a slinky out on a table, between your hands. Move one hand back and forth to shorten the end of the slinky. The shortened area moves along the slinky as a wave, but each coil only moves back and forth in the same place.

You hear sounds when sound waves reach your ears. The vibrating air makes your **ear drums** vibrate. Your ear turns these vibrations into signals that are sent to your brain.

Rest your hand on your throat while you speak. Can you feel vibrations?

REAL WORLD SCIENCE

Musical instruments make air vibrate in different ways. This is why they sound so different. To make an instrument you need something that vibrates when you tap, pluck, blow or scrape it. The vibrations are passed on through the air to our ears.

Make a Rice Puff Bop

Sounds are made when something **vibrates**. We can't always see the vibrations, for example when a mobile phone rings. Can you prove they are there?

EQUIPMENT

- A cell phone
- Large glass jar
- Plastic wrap
- Puffed rice cereal

Method

1 Set the cell phone to ring with a musical or ringing tone (make sure the "vibrate" mode is turned off). Put the phone inside an empty glass jar.

2 Stretch a piece of plastic wrap over the top of the jar, as tightly as possible. This is the dance floor for your rice puff bop.

3 Scatter a few pieces of puffed rice on the plastic wrap.

Predict: What do you think will happen to the puffed rice when the phone rings?

4 Call the cell phone so that it starts ringing. What happens to the puffed rice?

5 Repeat the **experiment**, turning up the **volume** of the phone each time. Does it change the way the puffed rice dances? What happens if you use different dancers, such as grains of salt?

IS IT A FAIR TEST?

To make it a fair test, you should only change one thing at a time. When you change the volume of the phone, is the plastic wrap stretched just as tightly each time? How could you improve your experiment?

Conclusion

When something makes a sound, part of it must be vibrating. Sometimes the vibrations are very small and hard to see. When the phone speaker vibrates, the air next to it vibrates, too. The vibrations are passed through the air and the sides of the container to the plastic wrap. The dancing puffed rice helps you to see the vibrations.

What Makes Sounds Loud or Soft?

Sound is a form of **energy**. When a sound passes through the air, energy is being transfered from place to place.

REAL WORLD SCIENCE

Sound energy can be changed into other forms of energy – and back again. This is useful. A microphone changes sound energy into **electrical signals**. These can travel farther than **sound waves** without fading. A loudspeaker changes electrical signals back into sound waves.

Volume and vibrations

The loudness or softness of a sound is called its **volume**. The volume of a sound wave tells us how much energy it has. A loud sound makes the air **vibrate** more, so more sound energy reaches our ears. Smaller vibrations mean that less sound energy reaches our ears, and the sound is quiet or soft.

When you pluck a rubber band, you transfer energy to it. The harder you pluck, the more energy you transfer and the bigger the vibrations. Bigger vibrations make louder sounds.

As sound waves travel, their energy fades and the sound becomes quieter. Because louder sounds have more energy to start with, they travel farther.

Sound energy is measured in **decibels**. Our ears can be damaged by too much sound energy.

REAL WORLD SCIENCE

A stethoscope focuses sound energy and sends it all in one direction, along a narrow pathway. This makes it possible to hear very quiet sounds, such as a heartbeat.

Turn Up the Volume

How can you make a quiet sound louder, and easier to hear? You could stand closer to the source, so the **sound waves** have more **energy** when they reach your ears. Is there another way?

EQUIPMENT

- Something that makes a very quiet sound, e.g. a ticking clock
- Large, medium, and small sheets of paper
- Large, quiet room
- Tape measure or metre rule
- Tape
- Scissors

Method

1. Stand next to the clock. Can you hear it ticking? Try moving a few feet away. Can you still hear it ticking? How far can you go before you stop hearing the clock?

2 Roll the smallest sheet of paper into a cone. Make the smallest opening about 1 inch (2.5 centimeters) across. Use a piece of tape to hold the cone together.

Predict: If you listen to the clock through the cone, will it sound louder, softer or the same?

3 Hold the smallest opening of the cone to your ear and listen to the clock. What do you hear? Does it sound louder, softer or the same? Move your head so that the cone points in different directions. Does this change how the clock sounds?

Don't put the end of the cone in your ear. Rest it just next to your ear.

4 Move 3 feet (one meter) away from the clock, and listen again. Record how far you can go before you stop hearing the clock through the cone.

5 Make a bigger cone, using the medium-sized sheet of paper. Hold it up to your ear and listen to the clock again. Does it sound louder or softer? Record how far you can go before you stop hearing the clock.

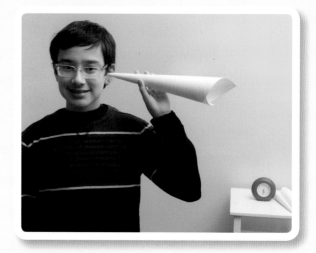

6 Make a cone using the largest sheet of paper. Use it to listen to the clock. Does it sound louder or softer? Record how far you can go before you stop hearing the clock through this cone.

7 Use a table like this to record your results. This will make it easier to compare them.

Hearing device	Distance when you stop hearing the clock (feet)
None	
Small cone	
Medium cone	
Large cone	

✓ IS IT A FAIR TEST?

Remember to change only one thing at a time – the **variable** you are testing. Everything else should stay the same. Is the original sound always the same? Is each cone made from the same type of paper? Is the smallest opening always 1 inch (3 centimeters) across?

Conclusion

Sound **energy** from the ticking clock is passed through the air in all directions. Only a small amount of it reaches your ears. A cone-shaped "ear trumpet" gathers more **sound waves** than your ear can. As the sound waves travel down the cone towards your ear, their energy is combined. This **amplifies** the sound (makes it louder). Bigger cone ends gather more sound energy, so the sound is amplified more.

REAL WORLD SCIENCE

Hiding inside curled leaves helps these bats hear better. The leaves make a cone shape. Calls from other bats are amplified as they travel into the leaves. By the time they reach the bottom, sounds are up to 10 **decibels** louder!

What Can Sounds Travel Through?

Sound needs something to travel through. Most sound **vibrations** travel to our ears through air (a **gas**), but sound can travel through **solids** and **liquids**, too.

Sound can't travel in a **vacuum** such as space. There is no air to pass on the vibrations. If this spaceship exploded, the astronaut would hear almost nothing.

Don't put your fingers inside your ears.

!

Hang a wire coat hanger on a long piece of string. Wrap the ends of the string around the first finger of each hand. Swing the hanger so that it taps a wall gently. What do you hear? Now hold the tips of your first fingers tightly against your ears. Swing the hanger so it taps the wall gently. What do you hear? Try this out with other objects.

When you tap the coat hanger, it vibrates and makes a sound. The way we hear the sound depends on which material the vibrations travel through to reach our ears.

Sounds travel better through solids than gases. When the vibrations travel through air, not many of them reach our ears. The sound is quiet. When the vibrations travel through string, more of them reach your ears so the sound is much louder.

How Fast Do Sounds Travel?

Sound travels at different speeds through different materials. It can travel much faster through **solids** and **liquids** than through air.

Sound travels faster in water than in air, so it can travel farther before it fades. The loud sounds made by blue whales can be heard by other whales up to 995 miles (1,600 kilometers) away, which is like you standing in New York City and hearing someone speaking in Panama City, Florida.

EXPERIMENT 3

Make a Telephone

Sound travels faster and farther through **solids** than it does through **liquids** and **gases**. But do some solids transmit sound better than others? Find out by making a string telephone using different materials.

EQUIPMENT

- Two paper or plastic cups
- Two paper clips
- Different materials such as yarn, string, thin metal wire, nylon fishing line, dental floss, and cotton thread.

Method

1. Ask an adult to help you measure and cut a 30 foot length of yarn. Ask an adult to make a small hole in the bottom of each cup. Push each end of the yarn through a cup and tie it to a paperclip to hold it in place.

ADULT HELP

2. Have a friend hold one cup while you hold the other. Move apart until the yarn is stretched tightly. Hold your cup to your ear while your friend speaks into the other cup. Can you hear them?

3 Ask your friend to choose ten words from a dictionary and speak them into their cup, in a quiet voice. Listen through your cup, and write down what you hear.

4 Repeat steps 1 and 3 using a different materials to join the cups.

Predict: Which material will be best at transmitting sound? Which will be worst?

Material	Predicted rank (1 = best at transmitting sound)	Number of words heard correctly	Actual rank
Air			
Yarn			
Metal wire			

5 Use a table like the one at the bottom of page 20 to record your results. Analyze your results. Which material made the best telephone?

IS IT A FAIR TEST?

Make sure you only change the **variable** you are testing. This is the material used to join the cups. The length and tightness of each cord should be the same. Is it a fair test if each material is a different thickness? Is your friend speaking at the same **volume** each time? Is it a fair test if your friend says different words each time? How could you improve your **experiment**?

Conclusion

When you speak into your telephone, the **sound waves** travel from the first cup to the second cup through the cord. Sound travels better through cords made of **denser** materials such as metal wire. Softer materials, such as yarn, **absorb** more sound than harder materials. The tightness of the cord also changes how well sound travels. Can you use this to explain your results?

What Makes Sounds High or Low?

Two sounds can be the same **volume**, but sound very different. Sounds can be low like a lion roaring, or high like a monkey screaming.

The **pitch** of a sound describes how high or low the sound is. It is linked to the number of **vibrations** (or **sound waves**) that reach our ears every second.

High sounds have a high number of sound waves per second.

Low sounds have a low number of sound waves per second.

Anything that affects how quickly an object vibrates can affect the pitch of the sound it makes.

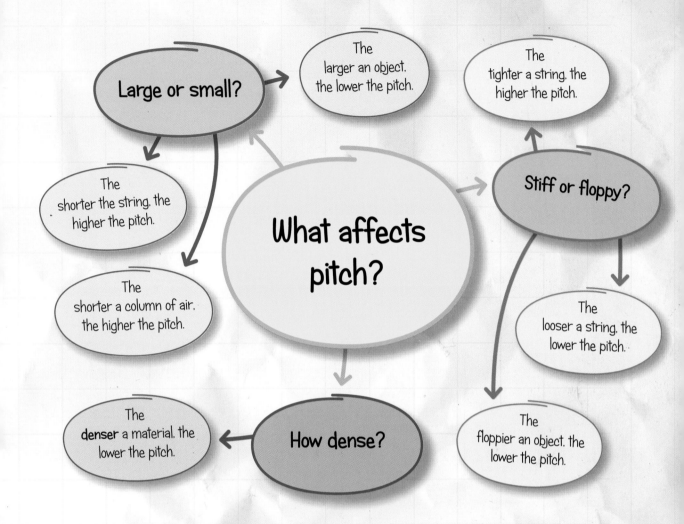

Large or small?

The larger an object, the lower the pitch.

The tighter a string, the higher the pitch.

The shorter the string, the higher the pitch.

What affects pitch?

Stiff or floppy?

The shorter a column of air, the higher the pitch.

The looser a string, the lower the pitch.

The denser a material, the lower the pitch.

How dense?

The floppier an object, the lower the pitch.

SEE THE SCIENCE ⤵

Wrap two rubber bands around an empty box. Wrap one around the box twice so it is tighter. Pluck both bands. The tighter band vibrates more quickly. It makes a higher pitched sound.

Bottle Band

Can you change the sound a bottle makes just by adding water? **Experiment** with changing **pitch** and make music.

EQUIPMENT

- Five empty glass bottles
- Measuring jug
- Water
- Wooden spoon
- Stickers numbered 1 to 5

Method

1 Fill one bottle with water and leave one empty. Pour a different amount of water into each of the others. This is your drum kit!

Predict: Which bottle will make the highest sound when you tap it, and which will make the lowest sound?

2 Put a sticker on each bottle to record your prediction—1 for the bottle that you think will make the highest sound, and 5 for the lowest sound.

Glass can be dangerous if it breaks. Ask an adult to help you.

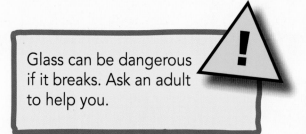

3 Tap the side of each bottle with a wooden spoon. What do you hear?

 4 Line up the bottles in order of pitch. Was your prediction right? How can you make a note lower or higher?

☑ IS IT A FAIR TEST?

The **variable** that you are changing is the amount of water in each bottle. Everything else should stay the same. Is it a **fair test** if the bottles are different shapes and sizes? Is it a fair test if they are standing on different surfaces? How can you improve your experiment?

5 Repeat the **experiment**, but this time blow across the top of each bottle instead of tapping it.

Predict: Which bottle will make the highest sound when you blow across it, and which will make the lowest sound?

6 Put a sticker on each bottle to record your prediction – 1 for the bottle that you think will make the highest sound, and 5 for the lowest sound.

7 Blow across the top of each bottle. What do you hear?

8 Line up the bottles in order of **pitch**. Was your prediction right? How can you make a note lower or higher?

Conclusion

When you tap the bottles with a wooden spoon, the glass and water **vibrate** together and make a sound. The fuller bottles have more **mass**, which wobbles more slowly. They produce lower sounds. The fullest bottle makes the lowest sound. The empty bottle makes the highest sound.

When you blow across the bottles, it is the air inside the bottles that vibrates to make the sound. A shorter column of air vibrates more quickly, so the bottles with most water make the highest sounds. The longer the column of air, the lower the **pitch**.

Try changing the amount of water in each bottle to match the pitch of notes played on an instrument. Then use your bottle band to play real tunes!

Plan Your Next Experiment

Experiments have helped you discover some amazing things about sound. Just like you, scientists carry out experiments to answer questions and test ideas. Each experiment is planned carefully to make it a **fair test**.

YOU ASKED...

YOU FOUND OUT THAT...

What causes sounds?

→

- Sounds are made when something **vibrates**. Sometimes the vibrations are too small to see.
- The vibrations make the air or material next to them vibrate, too.
- The vibrations are passed through a material as **sound waves**.

What makes sounds louder and softer?

→

- Sound is a form of **energy**. The more energy a sound wave has, the louder the sound.
- The bigger the vibration, the louder the sound.
- A cone-shaped "ear trumpet" focuses sounds toward your ears, and **amplifies** them (makes them louder).

What can sound travel through?

→

- Sound can travel through different materials, including **solids**, **liquids**, and **gases**.
- Sound travels through some materials better than others. This can be useful when you want to **muffle** a sound.

What makes sounds high or low?

→

- The **pitch** of a sound (how high or low it is) is related to the number of vibrations per second.
- Faster vibrations lead to higher pitch sounds.
- The tighter a vibrating string is, the higher the pitch of the sound.
- The larger a vibrating object is, the lower the pitch of the sound.

Experiments also lead to new questions! Did you think of more questions about sound? Can you plan new experiments to help answer them?

Being a scientist and carrying out experiments is exciting. What will you discover next?

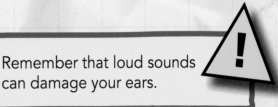

Remember that loud sounds can damage your ears.

WHAT NEXT?

→ Do the vibrations change if you change the tightness of the plastic wrap, or the material of the container or dance floor? Plan an experiment to find out.

→ Does the material of the ear trumpet make a difference? Plan an experiment to find out.

→ How well do different materials **absorb** or reflect sound? Plan an experiment to find out. Hint: Try making headphones stuffed with different materials.

→ What happens when you change the length, thickness or material of a vibrating cord? Plan experiments to find out.

Glossary

absorb soak up

amplify make louder

analyze examine the results of an experiment carefully, in order to explain what happened

decibel unit used to measure the volume of a sound; can be written as dB

dense how tightly packed the matter that makes up a material is

ear drum part of the ear that vibrates when sound waves hit it

electrical signals small bursts of electricity used to send coded information

energy the power to make something happen

experiment procedure carried out to test an idea or answer a question

gas material that changes shape to fill its container, and can expand or be compressed so it takes up a different amount of space

liquid material that is runny and changes shape to fill the bottom of its container, but always takes up the same amount of space

mass the amount of matter making up an object or material

muffle stop sound traveling; make a quieter sound

observation noting or measuring what you see, hear, smell or feel

pitch how high or low a sound is

prediction best guess or estimate of what will happen, based on what you already know

solid material that is firm, does not change shape and always takes up the same amount of space

sound wave how sound travels through air

vacuum completely empty space

variable something that can be changed

vibrate move back and forth very quickly

volume how loud or soft a sound is

Find Out More

Books

Riley, Peter. *Bang! Sound and How We Hear Things.* London, UK:
Franklin Watts, 2012

Spilsbury, Richard and Louise. *Making Noise! Making Sounds.* Chicago:
Heinemann Library, 2014

Spilsbury, Richard and Louise. *Shhh! Listen! Hearing Sounds.* Chicago:
Heinemann Library, 2014

Web sites

FactHound offers a safe, fun way to find internet sites
related to this book. All of the sites on FactHound have
been researched by our staff.

Here's all you do:
Visit www.facthound.com
Type in this code: 9781410968364

Index